# Weather in Winter

BY JENNA LEE GLEISNER

**The Child's World®**
childsworld.com

Published by The Child's World®
1980 Lookout Drive • Mankato, MN 56003-1705
800-599-READ • www.childsworld.com

Photographs ©: Ami Parikh/Shutterstock Images, cover, 1; MN Studio/Shutterstock Images, 4–5; Creative Travel Projects/Shutterstock Images, 6–7; iStockphoto, 9; Shutterstock Images, 10–11, 12–13, 15; Alexander Gold/Shutterstock Images, 16–17; Tijana Photography/Shutterstock Images, 18; Maxim Petrichuk/Shutterstock Images, 21; Red Line Editorial, 22

ISBN 9781503823907
LCCN 2017944880

Printed in the United States of America
PA02359

## ABOUT THE AUTHOR

Jenna Lee Gleisner is an author and editor who lives in Minnesota. She has written more than 80 books for children. When not writing or editing, she enjoys spending time with her family and her dog, Norrie.

# Contents

# Cold Weather

It is a cold winter day.

Snow falls.

Earth **tilts**. This makes the **seasons**. Part of Earth tilts away from the sun in winter.

Earth gets less sunlight in winter. Temperatures drop.

# Winter Storms

Cool air sinks. Warm air rises. This creates wind.

Winter storms are called **blizzards**. Wind blows the snow.

# Snow and Ice

Water **freezes** at cold temperatures. It becomes a **solid**.

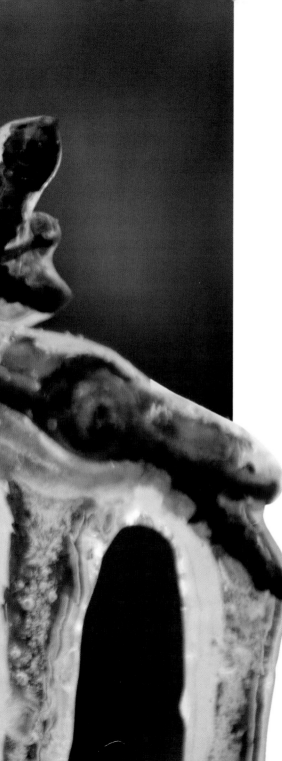

Rain turns to snow.
Rain and snow can
turn into ice.

Parts of ponds and lakes freeze. Ice forms on the **surface**.

Spring comes after winter.
Snow and ice will melt
in spring.

# Snowflake Ornaments

Make your own snowflake ornament!

**Supplies:**

4 popsicle sticks    glitter
  white paint    string
  paintbrush
  glue

**Instructions:**

1. Paint the popsicle sticks with white paint. Let them dry.

2. Dab glue onto the middle of one of the popsicle sticks. Place another stick on top so it forms a cross. Then glue the other sticks on diagonally.

3. Glue glitter onto your snowflake. After it is dry, tie a piece of string around it. Then hang your snowflake ornament wherever you would like!

# Glossary

**blizzards** — (BLIZ-urdz) Blizzards are snowstorms with strong winds. It can be hard to see during blizzards.

**freezes** — (FREEZ-uhz) A liquid freezes when it becomes very cold. A pond freezes in winter.

**seasons** — (SEE-zuhnz) Seasons are the four natural parts of the year. Winter is one of the seasons.

**solid** — (SAH-lid) A solid is something that is hard, unlike a liquid or a gas. When water freezes in winter, it becomes a solid.

**surface** — (SUR-fiss) A surface is the top layer of something. Ice forms on the surface of a lake in winter.

**tilts** — (TILTS) Something tilts when it leans to one side. Part of Earth tilts away from the sun during winter.

# To Learn More

## Books

Appleby, Alex. *What Happens in Winter?* New York, NY: Gareth Stevens Publishing, 2014.

Marino Walters, Jennifer. *Wonderful Winter.* Egremont, MA: Rocking Chair Kids, 2017.

## Web Sites

Visit our Web site for links about weather in winter:
**childsworld.com/links**

*Note to Parents, Teachers, and Librarians: We routinely verify our Web links to make sure they are safe and active sites. So encourage your readers to check them out!*

# Index